PERSONAL INFORMATION

Name:

Address:

Telephone: Email:

Employer:

Address:

Telephone: Email:

MEDICAL INFORMATION

Physician: Telephone:

Allergies:

Medications:

Blood Type:

Insurer:

IN CASE OF EMERGENCY, NOTIFY

Name:

Address:

Telephone: Relationship:

Published by Barbour Publishing, Inc., 1810 Barbour Drive, Uhrichsville, Ohio 44683, www.barbourbooks.com

Our mission is to inspire the world with the life-changing message of the Bible.

Member of the
Evangelical Christian
Publishers Association

Printed in China.

STRESS LESS PRAY MORE

2023 PLANNER

BARBOUR

PUBLISHING

STRESS LESS,
PRAY MORE!

*Make sure that you don't get so absorbed and
exhausted in taking care of all your day-by-day
obligations that you lose track of the time and doze
off, oblivious to God. . . . Be up and awake to what
God is doing! God is putting the finishing touches on
the salvation work he began when we first believed.*

ROMANS 13:11–12 MSG

Stress. We're anxious about everything from piles of laundry and doctors' bills, to job security and the economy. Amid all these worries, we are surrounded by the noise of technology and information overload. But God has a time-tested solution: prayer.

This delightful planner will help you plan the weeks and months of a brand-new year while living in God's freedom. Each page offers gentle, truth-filled reminders that when you focus wholly on Him, you can reconnect with the power and peace to live a calmer, wonder-filled life every day of the year!

YEAR at a GLANCE

JANUARY

S	M	T	W	T	F	S
1	2	3	4	5	6	7
8	9	10	11	12	13	14
15	16	17	18	19	20	21
22	23	24	25	26	27	28
29	30	31				

FEBRUARY

S	M	T	W	T	F	S
			1	2	3	4
5	6	7	8	9	10	11
12	13	14	15	16	17	18
19	20	21	22	23	24	25
26	27	28				

MAY

S	M	T	W	T	F	S
	1	2	3	4	5	6
7	8	9	10	11	12	13
14	15	16	17	18	19	20
21	22	23	24	25	26	27
28	29	30	31			

JUNE

S	M	T	W	T	F	S
				1	2	3
4	5	6	7	8	9	10
11	12	13	14	15	16	17
18	19	20	21	22	23	24
25	26	27	28	29	30	

SEPTEMBER

S	M	T	W	T	F	S
					1	2
3	4	5	6	7	8	9
10	11	12	13	14	15	16
17	18	19	20	21	22	23
24	25	26	27	28	29	30

OCTOBER

S	M	T	W	T	F	S
1	2	3	4	5	6	7
8	9	10	11	12	13	14
15	16	17	18	19	20	21
22	23	24	25	26	27	28
29	30	31				

2023

MARCH

S	M	T	W	T	F	S
			1	2	3	4
5	6	7	8	9	10	11
12	13	14	15	16	17	18
19	20	21	22	23	24	25
26	27	28	29	30	31	

APRIL

S	M	T	W	T	F	S
						1
2	3	4	5	6	7	8
9	10	11	12	13	14	15
16	17	18	19	20	21	22
23	24	25	26	27	28	29
30						

JULY

S	M	T	W	T	F	S
						1
2	3	4	5	6	7	8
9	10	11	12	13	14	15
16	17	18	19	20	21	22
23	24	25	26	27	28	29
30	31					

AUGUST

S	M	T	W	T	F	S
		1	2	3	4	5
6	7	8	9	10	11	12
13	14	15	16	17	18	19
20	21	22	23	24	25	26
27	28	29	30	31		

NOVEMBER

S	M	T	W	T	F	S
			1	2	3	4
5	6	7	8	9	10	11
12	13	14	15	16	17	18
19	20	21	22	23	24	25
26	27	28	29	30		

DECEMBER

S	M	T	W	T	F	S
					1	2
3	4	5	6	7	8	9
10	11	12	13	14	15	16
17	18	19	20	21	22	23
24	25	26	27	28	29	30
31						

AUGUST 2022

SUNDAY	MONDAY	TUESDAY	WEDNESDAY
31	1	2	3
7	8	9	10
14	15	16	17
21	22	23	24
28	29	30	31

THURSDAY	FRIDAY	SATURDAY
4	5	6
11	12	13
18	19	20
25	26	27
1	2	3

JULY

S	M	T	W	T	F	S
					1	2
3	4	5	6	7	8	9
10	11	12	13	14	15	16
17	18	19	20	21	22	23
24	25	26	27	28	29	30
31						

SEPTEMBER

S	M	T	W	T	F	S
				1	2	3
4	5	6	7	8	9	10
11	12	13	14	15	16	17
18	19	20	21	22	23	24
25	26	27	28	29	30	

ATTUNED TO GOD

How many times do we not let God in on our plans, run ahead of what He has planned, and miss the blessings He's waiting to pour out on us?

Perhaps it's time to stop trying to figure things out on our own, thinking we know best. Maybe our thoughts and feet should come to a screeching halt. This just might be the day we get it right.

Consider spending some time in the Word and in prayer, allowing God to lead the way. Know that, with God on your side, everything is and will be fine. Open up your mind to the wisdom and insight He has for you. Store His words in your heart. Then, and only then, attuned to and in step with Him, walk on.

Lord, I'm so tired of trying to do all this on my own. Show me what You would have me do, be, and see.

GOALS for this MONTH

- [ ] ....
- [ ] ....
- [ ] ....
- [ ] ....
- [ ] ....
- [ ] ....
- [ ] ....
- [ ] ....
- [ ] ....
- [ ] ....
- [ ] ....
- [ ] ....
- [ ] ....

*"Give in to God, come to terms with him and
everything will turn out just fine. Let him tell
you what to do; take his words to heart."*

JOB 22:21–22 MSG

JULY–AUGUST 2022

I'm here, Lord, limp in Your arms.
Please fill me with Your peace.

SUNDAY, July 31

....

....

....

....

MONDAY, August 1

....

....

....

....

TUESDAY, August 2

....

....

....

....

WEDNESDAY, August 3

THURSDAY, August 4

FRIDAY, August 5

SATURDAY, August 6

*"Let not your hearts be troubled. Believe in God;
believe also in me. . . . Peace I leave with you;
my peace I give to you. Not as the world
gives do I give to you. Let not your hearts
be troubled, neither let them be afraid."*

JOHN 14:1, 27 ESV

AUGUST 2022

Lord, give me the wisdom to watch my way,
knowing You have already gone before me and
made the path safe for my feet—and heart.

SUNDAY, August 7

....

....

....

....

MONDAY, August 8

....

....

....

....

TUESDAY, August 9

....

....

....

....

WEDNESDAY, August 10

....

....

....

....

THURSDAY, August 11

....

....

....

....

FRIDAY, August 12

....

....

....

....

SATURDAY, August 13

....

....

....

....

*Let your eyes look right on [with fixed purpose],
and let your gaze be straight before you.*
PROVERBS 4:25 AMPC

AUGUST 2022

Thank You, Lord, for providing for
me no matter where I go.

SUNDAY, August 14

MONDAY, August 15

TUESDAY, August 16

WEDNESDAY, August 17

....
....
....
....

THURSDAY, August 18

....
....
....
....

FRIDAY, August 19

....
....
....
....

SATURDAY, August 20

....
....
....
....

*"Arise and eat, for the journey
is too great for you."*
1 KINGS 19:7 ESV

AUGUST 2022

I'm focused on Your power, Lord.
Help me face whatever lies ahead.

SUNDAY, August 21

MONDAY, August 22

TUESDAY, August 23

WEDNESDAY, August 24

....

....

....

....

THURSDAY, August 25

....

....

....

....

FRIDAY, August 26

....

....

....

....

SATURDAY, August 27

....

....

....

....

*"Go back the way you came
through the desert."*
1 KINGS 19:15 MSG

Lord, here I am. Tell me what to do.

SUNDAY, August 28

MONDAY, August 29

TUESDAY, August 30

WEDNESDAY, August 31

THURSDAY, September 1

FRIDAY, September 2

SATURDAY, September 3

Trust GOD from the bottom of your heart; don't try to figure out everything on your own. Listen for GOD's voice in everything you do, everywhere you go; he's the one who will keep you on track.
PROVERBS 3:5-6 MSG

SEPTEMBER 2022

SUNDAY	MONDAY	TUESDAY	WEDNESDAY
28	29	30	31
4	5 _Labor Day_	6	7
11	12	13	14
18	19	20	21
25	26	27	28

THURSDAY	FRIDAY	SATURDAY
1	2	3
8	9	10
15	16	17
22	23	24
29 *First Day of Autumn*	30	1

FOLLOW HIM

Jesus was up against a lot of different political and religious factions. He was pressed by the crowds that were seeking healing physically, emotionally, mentally, and spiritually. He was teaching and training disciples who just didn't seem to get it right. He was pressured by Satan, who was trying to tempt Him away from His mission. He encountered people in His own hometown—even family members—who either didn't believe Him or wanted Him to tip His hand before it was time.

Yet in spite of all the things He was up against, Jesus never panicked but kept His peace. How? He went off alone and sought His Father God. He left the crowds and went to a deserted and desolate place. Somewhere secluded where He could meet with God one-on-one in the quiet of the morning hours.

Follow Him.

Lord, I come to You now,
alone, seeking Your face.

GOALS for this MONTH

- [ ] ....
- [ ] ....
- [ ] ....
- [ ] ....
- [ ] ....
- [ ] ....
- [ ] ....
- [ ] ....
- [ ] ....
- [ ] ....
- [ ] ....
- [ ] ....
- [ ] ....

*And rising very early in the morning, while
it was still dark, he departed and went out
to a desolate place, and there he prayed.*

MARK 1:35 ESV

SEPTEMBER 2022

Give me light for my path, Lord.
I'm not moving until You speak.

SUNDAY, September 4

....

....

....

....

MONDAY, September 5   *Labor Day*

....

....

....

....

TUESDAY, September 6

....

....

....

....

WEDNESDAY, September 7

....

....

....

....

THURSDAY, September 8

....

....

....

....

FRIDAY, September 9

....

....

....

....

SATURDAY, September 10

....

....

....

....

Then Jehoshaphat said to the king of Israel,
"But first, find out what the LORD's
word is in this matter."
1 KINGS 22:5 GW

SEPTEMBER 2022

Lord, help me to find joy wherever I
land, knowing You're there, helping me
not just to survive but to thrive!

SUNDAY, September 11

....
....
....
....

MONDAY, September 12

....
....
....
....

TUESDAY, September 13

....
....
....
....

WEDNESDAY, September 14

THURSDAY, September 15

FRIDAY, September 16

SATURDAY, September 17

When troubles of any kind come your way,
consider it an opportunity for great joy.
JAMES 1:2 NLT

SEPTEMBER 2022

Thank You, God, that I don't need to have all
the answers—because You have them for me!

SUNDAY, September 18

....

....

....

....

MONDAY, September 19

....

....

....

TUESDAY, September 20

....

....

....

....

WEDNESDAY, September 21

THURSDAY, September 22   *First Day of Autumn*

FRIDAY, September 23

SATURDAY, September 24

*We have no might to stand against this great
company that is coming against us. We do not
know what to do, but our eyes are upon You.*
2 Chronicles 20:12 ampc

SEPTEMBER-OCTOBER 2022

I find my freedom in You, Lord Jesus.

SUNDAY, September 25

MONDAY, September 26

TUESDAY, September 27

WEDNESDAY, September 28

THURSDAY, September 29

FRIDAY, September 30

SATURDAY, October 1

*Jesus said to those Jews who had believed in
Him, If you abide in My word [hold fast to My
teachings and live in accordance with them],
you are truly My disciples. And you will know
the Truth, and the Truth will set you free.*

JOHN 8:31–32 AMPC

OCTOBER 2022

SUNDAY	MONDAY	TUESDAY	WEDNESDAY
25	26	27	28
2	3	4	5
9	10 *Columbus Day*	11	12
16	17	18	19
23	24	25	26
30	*Halloween* 31		

THURSDAY	FRIDAY	SATURDAY
29	30	1
6	7	8
13	14	15
20	21	22
27	28	29

SEPTEMBER

S	M	T	W	T	F	S
				1	2	3
4	5	6	7	8	9	10
11	12	13	14	15	16	17
18	19	20	21	22	23	24
25	26	27	28	29	30	

NOVEMBER

S	M	T	W	T	F	S
		1	2	3	4	5
6	7	8	9	10	11	12
13	14	15	16	17	18	19
20	21	22	23	24	25	26
27	28	29	30			

ENLIGHTENED EYES OF FAITH

The Old Testament Joseph easily could have considered himself a victim of his circumstances and the people in his life. He could have blamed his brothers for throwing him into a pit and selling him to traders. He could have blamed Potiphar and his wife for his imprisonment. He could have blamed the baker and the wine bearer for leaving him to dream in the dark dungeon. But he never did. Instead, he persevered, believing that God, the Ruler of the universe, was with him, would protect him, and would turn his trials into triumphs. And so He did.

How would your outlook change if you realized that all things, people, and situations—both wonderful and awful—are part of God's plan for your life and that He will be with you through it all? Only through the enlightened eyes of your faith will you see God's caring hand in the world's darkness.

Thank You, God, for working out
Your good will in all things and
sticking with me through it all.

GOALS for this MONTH

- [ ] ....
- [ ] ....
- [ ] ....
- [ ] ....
- [ ] ....
- [ ] ....
- [ ] ....
- [ ] ....
- [ ] ....
- [ ] ....
- [ ] ....
- [ ] ....
- [ ] ....

"It wasn't you who sent me here, but God."
GENESIS 45:8 GW

I pause, Lord, to accept my feelings, align my thoughts with Yours, and live in Your truth.

SUNDAY, October 2

MONDAY, October 3

TUESDAY, October 4

WEDNESDAY, October 5

THURSDAY, October 6

FRIDAY, October 7

SATURDAY, October 8

The LORD is my light and my salvation.
Who is there to fear?
PSALM 27:1 GW

OCTOBER 2022

Lord, here I am. At Your feet.
Leaning back into Your presence.

SUNDAY, October 9

....
....
....
....

MONDAY, October 10   *Columbus Day*

....
....
....

TUESDAY, October 11

....
....
....
....

WEDNESDAY, October 12

....

....

....

....

THURSDAY, October 13

....

....

....

....

FRIDAY, October 14

....

....

....

....

SATURDAY, October 15

....

....

....

....

> *"Martha, Martha, you are anxious and troubled about many things, but one thing is necessary. Mary has chosen the good portion, which will not be taken away from her."*
>
> LUKE 10:41–42 ESV

OCTOBER 2022

Here I am, Lord, coming before You, seeking Your presence, breathing in Your Spirit, drinking in Your light, feeding on Your wisdom. Show me Your way.

SUNDAY, October 16

MONDAY, October 17

TUESDAY, October 18

WEDNESDAY, October 19

THURSDAY, October 20

FRIDAY, October 21

SATURDAY, October 22

You have said, Seek My face [inquire for and require My presence as your vital need]. My heart says to You, Your face (Your presence), Lord, will I seek, inquire for, and require [of necessity and on the authority of Your Word].

PSALM 27:8 AMPC

OCTOBER 2022

Thank You, Lord, for Your heavenly protection.

SUNDAY, October 23

MONDAY, October 24

TUESDAY, October 25

WEDNESDAY, October 26

....

....

....

....

THURSDAY, October 27

....

....

....

....

FRIDAY, October 28

....

....

....

....

SATURDAY, October 29

....

....

....

....

*He will give His angels [especial] charge over
you to accompany and defend and preserve
you in all your ways [of obedience and service].
They shall bear you up on their hands.*
PSALM 91:11–12 AMPC

NOVEMBER 2022

SUNDAY	MONDAY	TUESDAY	WEDNESDAY
30	31	1	2
6 *Daylight Saving Time Ends*	7	8 *Election Day*	9
13	14	15	16
20	21	22	23
27	28	29	30

THURSDAY	FRIDAY	SATURDAY
3	4	5
10	11 *Veterans Day*	12
17	18	19
24 *Thanksgiving Day*	25	26
1	2	3

OCTOBER

S	M	T	W	T	F	S
						1
2	3	4	5	6	7	8
9	10	11	12	13	14	15
16	17	18	19	20	21	22
23	24	25	26	27	28	29
30	31					

DECEMBER

S	M	T	W	T	F	S
				1	2	3
4	5	6	7	8	9	10
11	12	13	14	15	16	17
18	19	20	21	22	23	24
25	26	27	28	29	30	31

COUNTER ACTS

Studies have shown that keeping a gratitude journal reduces your stress! That's because people who count their blessings are more focused on how good things are. These "counter acts" naturally counteract stress, making blessing counters more resilient and more able to face whatever comes their way!

When was the last time you thanked God? What did you thank Him for? How can you make counting your blessings part of your regular routine?

Consider listing at least five things you're grateful for before going to bed at night. Doing so will not only make you a more optimistic, content, and joyful person, but it will help you sleep better!

Lord of my life, my heart rejoices in
You as my lips thank You for. . .

GOALS for this MONTH

- [ ] ....
- [ ] ....
- [ ] ....
- [ ] ....
- [ ] ....
- [ ] ....
- [ ] ....
- [ ] ....
- [ ] ....
- [ ] ....
- [ ] ....
- [ ] ....

"Oh, how my soul praises the Lord. How my spirit rejoices in God my Savior! For he took notice of his lowly servant girl. . . . For the Mighty One is holy, and he has done great things for me. . . . His mighty arm has done tremendous things!"

LUKE 1:46–48, 49, 51 NLT

OCTOBER-NOVEMBER 2022

Lord, I'm looking to You to help me navigate these
waters. I commit all my plans and works to You.

SUNDAY, October 30

MONDAY, October 31   *Halloween*

TUESDAY, November 1

WEDNESDAY, November 2

THURSDAY, November 3

FRIDAY, November 4

SATURDAY, November 5

Commit your actions to the Lord,
and your plans will succeed.
PROVERBS 16:3 NLT

NOVEMBER 2022

Jesus, I feel as if I'm slipping, falling.
Grab on to me. Never let me go.

SUNDAY, November 6   *Daylight Saving Time Ends*

MONDAY, November 7

TUESDAY, November 8   *Election Day*

WEDNESDAY, November 9

THURSDAY, November 10

FRIDAY, November 11   *Veterans Day*

SATURDAY, November 12

The minute I said, "I'm slipping, I'm falling,"
your love, GOD, took hold and held me fast.
When I was upset and beside myself, you
calmed me down and cheered me up.
PSALM 94:18–19 MSG

Thank You, Lord,
for loving me just the way I am.

SUNDAY, November 13

MONDAY, November 14

TUESDAY, November 15

WEDNESDAY, November 16

THURSDAY, November 17

FRIDAY, November 18

SATURDAY, November 19

"Don't be afraid; you are more valuable to God than a whole flock of sparrows."
MATTHEW 10:31 NLT

NOVEMBER 2022

Show me, Lord, what passion I can pursue
that can, at the same time, serve others—
in Your love and name!

SUNDAY, November 20

MONDAY, November 21

TUESDAY, November 22

WEDNESDAY, November 23

THURSDAY, November 24   *Thanksgiving Day*

FRIDAY, November 25

SATURDAY, November 26

*Let's see how inventive we can be in encouraging
love and helping out, not avoiding worshiping
together as some do but spurring each other on.*
HEBREWS 10:24–25 MSG

Lord, I'm stuck in a bad-news rut.
Help me focus on Your healing joy.

SUNDAY, November 27

MONDAY, November 28

TUESDAY, November 29

WEDNESDAY, November 30

THURSDAY, December 1

FRIDAY, December 2

SATURDAY, December 3

A cheerful disposition is good for your health;
gloom and doom leave you bone-tired.
PROVERBS 17:22 MSG

DECEMBER 2022

SUNDAY	MONDAY	TUESDAY	WEDNESDAY
27	28	29	30
4	5	6	7
11	12	13	14
18	19	20	21
Hanukkah Begins at Sundown			*First Day of Winter*
25	26	27	28
Christmas Day			

THURSDAY	FRIDAY	SATURDAY
1	2	3
8	9	10
15	16	17
22	23	24 *Christmas Eve*
29	30	31 *New Year's Eve*

NOVEMBER

S	M	T	W	T	F	S
		1	2	3	4	5
6	7	8	9	10	11	12
13	14	15	16	17	18	19
20	21	22	23	24	25	26
27	28	29	30			

JANUARY

S	M	T	W	T	F	S
1	2	3	4	5	6	7
8	9	10	11	12	13	14
15	16	17	18	19	20	21
22	23	24	25	26	27	28
29	30	31				

FAITH, LOVE, AND HOPE

The prayers of those who have gone before us are continually before God (see Revelation 5:8; 8:3). *And* the prayers of our loved ones stick to us like gum on a hot sidewalk. As Abraham Lincoln said, "I remember my mother's prayers and they have always followed me. They have clung to me all my life."

Not only do you have the prayer power to cover your own loved ones, but saints, such as the apostle Paul, have used their prayer power to cover *you*. Be encouraged by this. Know that because of your faith, great things are happening and will happen in your life. Know that others are grateful for your labors in love.

Relax and tap into the timelessness of faith, love, and hope.

Thank You, Jesus, for the faith, love,
and hope with which You bless me.

GOALS for this MONTH

- [ ] ....
- [ ] ....
- [ ] ....
- [ ] ....
- [ ] ....
- [ ] ....
- [ ] ....
- [ ] ....
- [ ] ....
- [ ] ....
- [ ] ....
- [ ] ....

*We give thanks to God always for all of you,
constantly mentioning you in our prayers,
remembering before our God and Father
your work of faith and labor of love and
steadfastness of hope in our Lord Jesus Christ.*

1 THESSALONIANS 1:2-3 ESV

DECEMBER 2022

Help me, Lord, to stop and straighten up my
life every once in a while. I know doing so will
be time spent in a worthy pursuit of peace.

SUNDAY, December 4

MONDAY, December 5

TUESDAY, December 6

WEDNESDAY, December 7

....

....

....

....

THURSDAY, December 8

....

....

....

....

FRIDAY, December 9

....

....

....

....

SATURDAY, December 10

....

....

....

....

For God is not a God of disorder but of peace.
1 CORINTHIANS 14:33 NLT

DECEMBER 2022

Lord, help me to be there for You,
myself, and others. Be the reigning
power in my life once again!

SUNDAY, December 11

MONDAY, December 12

TUESDAY, December 13

WEDNESDAY, December 14

THURSDAY, December 15

FRIDAY, December 16

SATURDAY, December 17

*Let us also lay aside every weight. . .looking to
Jesus, the founder and perfecter of our faith.*
HEBREWS 12:1–2 ESV

DECEMBER 2022

Lord, help me to continually love and look for
the best in everyone, just as You do for me.

SUNDAY, December 18   *Hanukkah Begins at Sundown*

....

....

....

....

MONDAY, December 19

....

....

....

....

TUESDAY, December 20

....

....

....

....

WEDNESDAY, December 21   *First Day of Winter*

....

....

....

....

THURSDAY, December 22

....

....

....

....

FRIDAY, December 23

....

....

....

....

SATURDAY, December 24   *Christmas Eve*

....

....

....

....

*"I'm telling you to love your enemies. Let them
bring out the best in you, not the worst. When
someone gives you a hard time, respond with the
supple moves of prayer, for then you are working
out of your true selves, your God-created selves."*
MATTHEW 5:44–45 MSG

DECEMBER 2022

I know You will give me all the wisdom I desire, Lord. Walk with me. Talk to me. I await Your direction with patience and trust.

SUNDAY, December 25   *Christmas Day*

....

....

....

....

MONDAY, December 26

....

....

....

....

TUESDAY, December 27

....

....

....

....

WEDNESDAY, December 28

THURSDAY, December 29

FRIDAY, December 30

SATURDAY, December 31   *New Year's Eve*

*Such things were written in the Scriptures
long ago to teach us. And the Scriptures
give us hope and encouragement as we wait
patiently for God's promises to be fulfilled.*
ROMANS 15:4 NLT

JANUARY 2023

SUNDAY	MONDAY	TUESDAY	WEDNESDAY
1 *New Year's Day*	2	3	4
8	9	10	11
15	16 *Marin Luther King Jr. Day*	17	18
22	23	24	25
29	30	31	1

THURSDAY	FRIDAY	SATURDAY
5	6	7
12	13	14
19	20	21
26	27	28
2	3	4

DECEMBER

S	M	T	W	T	F	S
				1	2	3
4	5	6	7	8	9	10
11	12	13	14	15	16	17
18	19	20	21	22	23	24
25	26	27	28	29	30	31

FEBRUARY

S	M	T	W	T	F	S
			1	2	3	4
5	6	7	8	9	10	11
12	13	14	15	16	17	18
19	20	21	22	23	24	25
26	27	28				

CAUGHT UP

Sometimes we get so caught up in our lives, so stressed out, that we don't recognize where God may be directing our attention, the solutions He might be providing if only we'd look or listen, whether through circumstances, prayer, the wisdom of others, or the scriptures.

Consider how Jesus was preaching one day from Simon's boat after a long night of unsuccessful fishing on the part of Simon and his crew. Yet at Jesus' word, Simon lowered his nets—and brought up a bounty of fish.

Are you awake and open to what God is saying? Where might He be telling you to let down your net?

Lord, I come before You, my eyes and ears open. What would You have me do?

GOALS for this MONTH

- ☐ ....
- ☐ ....
- ☐ ....
- ☐ ....
- ☐ ....
- ☐ ....
- ☐ ....
- ☐ ....
- ☐ ....
- ☐ ....
- ☐ ....
- ☐ ....

Simon answered, "Master, we toiled all night and took nothing! But at your word I will let down the nets." And when they had done this, they enclosed a large number of fish, and their nets were breaking.

LUKE 5:5–6 ESV

JANUARY 2023

Lord, help me to pray, ponder, and put myself
in Your hands as You speak to my heart.

SUNDAY, January 1   *New Year's Day*

....

....

....

....

MONDAY, January 2

....

....

....

....

TUESDAY, January 3

....

....

....

....

WEDNESDAY, January 4

....
....
....
....

THURSDAY, January 5

....
....
....
....

FRIDAY, January 6

....
....
....
....

SATURDAY, January 7

....
....
....
....

*Mary was keeping within herself
all these things (sayings), weighing and
pondering them in her heart.*
LUKE 2:19 AMPC

JANUARY 2023

Help me, Lord, to seek and be open to
Your vision in every situation I face.

SUNDAY, January 8

MONDAY, January 9

TUESDAY, January 10

WEDNESDAY, January 11

....

....

....

....

THURSDAY, January 12

....

....

....

....

FRIDAY, January 13

....

....

....

....

SATURDAY, January 14

....

....

....

....

> *The LORD said to Samuel, "Don't judge by his*
> *appearance or height, for I have rejected him.*
> *The LORD doesn't see things the way you see*
> *them. People judge by outward appearance,*
> *but the LORD looks at the heart."*
>
> 1 SAMUEL 16:7 NLT

JANUARY 2023

Lord, help me be a woman who follows
the Rule Giver more than the rules. Help
me be a woman after Your own heart.

SUNDAY, January 15

MONDAY, January 16   *Martin Luther King Jr. Day*

TUESDAY, January 17

WEDNESDAY, January 18

THURSDAY, January 19

FRIDAY, January 20

SATURDAY, January 21

"God removed Saul and replaced him with David,
a man about whom God said, 'I have found
David son of Jesse, a man after my own heart.
He will do everything I want him to do.'"
ACTS 13:22 NLT

JANUARY 2023

I come to You, Lord, with my whole heart.

SUNDAY, January 22

....
....
....
....

MONDAY, January 23

....
....
....
....

TUESDAY, January 24

....
....
....
....

WEDNESDAY, January 25

THURSDAY, January 26

FRIDAY, January 27

SATURDAY, January 28

*Then you will seek Me, inquire for, and require
Me [as a vital necessity] and find Me when
you search for Me with all your heart.*
JEREMIAH 29:13 AMPC

FEBRUARY 2023

SUNDAY	MONDAY	TUESDAY	WEDNESDAY
29	30	31	1
5	6	7	8
12	13	14 *Valentine's Day*	15
19	20 *Presidents Day*	21	22 *Ash Wednesday*
26	27	28	1

THURSDAY	FRIDAY	SATURDAY
2	3	4
9	10	11
16	17	18
23	24	25
2	3	4

JANUARY

S	M	T	W	T	F	S
1	2	3	4	5	6	7
8	9	10	11	12	13	14
15	16	17	18	19	20	21
22	23	24	25	26	27	28
29	30	31				

MARCH

S	M	T	W	T	F	S
			1	2	3	4
5	6	7	8	9	10	11
12	13	14	15	16	17	18
19	20	21	22	23	24	25
26	27	28	29	30	31	

CLOSE TO HIS HEART

You are in the Great Shepherd's arms. You have no need to fear. To struggle. To panic. You are in the safest place you could ever be. In the arms of the One who loves you beyond compare, who sacrificed His life so that you could be with Him forever. He is watching over you. He's the barrier between you and that which could harm you. He is the One who meets all your needs. He leads you down the right paths, to clean, living water and food that satisfies.

So be still. Relax in His arms. Lean back. Breathe deep. Feel His heartbeat. You are home. Let Him carry you.

Lord, here I am, leaning back against You, listening to Your heartbeat, feeling Your breath and the warmth of Your love. Hold me tight. Keep me close forevermore.

GOALS for this MONTH

- [ ] ....
- [ ] ....
- [ ] ....
- [ ] ....
- [ ] ....
- [ ] ....
- [ ] ....
- [ ] ....
- [ ] ....
- [ ] ....
- [ ] ....
- [ ] ....
- [ ] ....

He will feed his flock like a shepherd.
He will carry the lambs in his arms,
holding them close to his heart.
ISAIAH 40:11 NLT

JANUARY–FEBRUARY 2023

Help me, Lord, to remember to keep my
thoughts on good things, like You, to rise
above the stresses and into Your light.

SUNDAY, January 29

....

....

....

....

MONDAY, January 30

....

....

....

TUESDAY, January 31

....

....

....

WEDNESDAY, February 1

....

....

....

....

THURSDAY, February 2

....

....

....

....

FRIDAY, February 3

....

....

....

....

SATURDAY, February 4

....

....

....

....

*Fix your thoughts on what is true,
and honorable, and right, and pure, and
lovely, and admirable. Think about things
that are excellent and worthy of praise.*
PHILIPPIANS 4:8 NLT

FEBRUARY 2023

Lord, I'm returning for rest in You today.

SUNDAY, February 5

....
....
....
....

MONDAY, February 6

....
....
....
....

TUESDAY, February 7

....
....
....
....

WEDNESDAY, February 8

....

....

....

....

THURSDAY, February 9

....

....

....

....

FRIDAY, February 10

....

....

....

....

SATURDAY, February 11

....

....

....

....

*The Sovereign LORD. . .says: "Only in returning
to me and resting in me will you be saved.
In quietness and confidence is your strength." . . .
Your own ears will hear him. Right behind you
a voice will say, "This is the way you should
go," whether to the right or to the left.*
ISAIAH 30:15, 21 NLT

FEBRUARY 2023

I am Your breath within a body,
Lord. Help me live Your way.

SUNDAY, February 12

MONDAY, February 13

TUESDAY, February 14 *Valentine's Day*

WEDNESDAY, February 15

THURSDAY, February 16

FRIDAY, February 17

SATURDAY, February 18

*So those who received his word were baptized,
and there were added that day about three thousand
souls. And they devoted themselves to the apostles'
teaching and the fellowship, to the breaking of bread
and the prayers. And awe came upon every soul.*
ACTS 2:41–43 ESV

Thank You, Lord, for being the one and
only true God. Help me be still in You.

SUNDAY, February 19

MONDAY, February 20   *Presidents Day*

TUESDAY, February 21

WEDNESDAY, February 22   *Ash Wednesday*

THURSDAY, February 23

FRIDAY, February 24

SATURDAY, February 25

*God is our refuge and strength, a very present
help in trouble. Therefore we will not fear
though the earth gives way, though the
mountains be moved into the heart of the sea.*
PSALM 46:1–2 ESV

FEBRUARY-MARCH 2023

Lord, I know You are amazing. Hear and see me.
Help me, so that all will know You alone are God!

SUNDAY, February 26

MONDAY, February 27

TUESDAY, February 28

WEDNESDAY, March 1

THURSDAY, March 2

FRIDAY, March 3

SATURDAY, March 4

*"Incline your ear, O LORD, and hear;
open your eyes, O LORD, and see."*
2 KINGS 19:16 ESV

MARCH 2023

SUNDAY	MONDAY	TUESDAY	WEDNESDAY
26	27	28	1
5	6	7	8
12 *Daylight Saving Time Begins*	13	14	15
19	20 *First Day of Spring*	21	22
26	27	28	29

THURSDAY	FRIDAY	SATURDAY
2	3	4
9	10	11
16	17	18
	St. Patrick's Day	
23	24	25
30	31	1

FEBRUARY

S	M	T	W	T	F	S
				1	2	3	4
5	6	7	8	9	10	11
12	13	14	15	16	17	18
19	20	21	22	23	24	25
26	27	28				

APRIL

S	M	T	W	T	F	S
						1
2	3	4	5	6	7	8
9	10	11	12	13	14	15
16	17	18	19	20	21	22
23	24	25	26	27	28	29
30						

YOUR VERY BREATH

God is not some distant, foreign deity. He is closer than your very breath. St. Gregory of Nazianzus advised us, "Remember God more often than you breathe."

Imagine thinking of God with each inhale and exhale. Pause in this moment and feel that breath. Feel God's presence. Recognize He is above, below, within, and without. With these ideas at the forefront of your mind and the awareness of His love in the depths of your soul, there is no room for fight, flight, or freeze. There is simply peace as you live, move, and have your being.

Lord, You are not some piece of wood or stone. You are a living God who is working in my life, taking care of me, and bringing me peace and contentment in this very moment as I live and breathe. In Jesus' name, amen.

GOALS for this MONTH

- [ ] ....
- [ ] ....
- [ ] ....
- [ ] ....
- [ ] ....
- [ ] ....
- [ ] ....
- [ ] ....
- [ ] ....
- [ ] ....
- [ ] ....
- [ ] ....
- [ ] ....

*They should seek God, in the hope that they
might feel after Him and find Him, although
He is not far from each one of us. For in Him
we live and move and have our being.*

ACTS 17:27–28 AMPC

Help me to have the faith and trust of a
three-year-old, Lord. Help me to see that,
with You right next to me, it'll be fine.

SUNDAY, March 5

MONDAY, March 6

TUESDAY, March 7

WEDNESDAY, March 8

....

....

....

....

THURSDAY, March 9

....

....

....

....

FRIDAY, March 10

....

....

....

....

SATURDAY, March 11

....

....

....

....

> *The LORD replied, "I will personally go*
> *with you. . .and I will give you rest—*
> *everything will be fine for you."*
> EXODUS 33:14 NLT

MARCH 2023

I want to tap into Your power, Lord.
I know nothing is too hard or impossible
for You. Help me to have a strong
prayer life that breaks chains.

SUNDAY, March 12 *Daylight Saving Time Begins*

MONDAY, March 13

TUESDAY, March 14

WEDNESDAY, March 15

THURSDAY, March 16

FRIDAY, March 17   *St. Patrick's Day*

SATURDAY, March 18

Paul and Silas were praying and singing hymns to God. . . . Suddenly, there was a massive earthquake, and the prison was shaken to its foundations. All the doors immediately flew open, and the chains of every prisoner fell off!
Acts 16:25-26 nlt

MARCH 2023

Lord, I pour out my heart to You right
now, holding nothing back. Free me!

SUNDAY, March 19

MONDAY, March 20   *First Day of Spring*

TUESDAY, March 21

WEDNESDAY, March 22

THURSDAY, March 23

FRIDAY, March 24

SATURDAY, March 25

*GOD met me more than halfway, he freed me
from my anxious fears. Look at him; give him
your warmest smile. Never hide your feelings
from him. When I was desperate, I called
out, and GOD got me out of a tight spot.*

PSALM 34:4–6 MSG

I see no way out of this situation,
Lord, but I know You do. And I trust
in You. I have peace in You.

SUNDAY, March 26

MONDAY, March 27

TUESDAY, March 28

WEDNESDAY, March 29

THURSDAY, March 30

FRIDAY, March 31

SATURDAY, April 1

> God's angel sets up a circle of protection around
> us while we pray. Open your mouth and taste, open
> your eyes and see—how good God is. Blessed are
> you who run to him. Worship God if you want the
> best; worship opens doors to all his goodness.
>
> PSALM 34:7–9 MSG

APRIL 2023

SUNDAY	MONDAY	TUESDAY	WEDNESDAY
26	27	28	29
2 *Palm Sunday*	3	4	5 *Passover Begins at Sundown*
9 *Easter*	10	11	12
16	17	18	19
23 30	24	25	26

THURSDAY	FRIDAY	SATURDAY
30	31	1
6	7 *Good Friday*	8
13	14	15
20	21	22
27	28	29

MARCH

S	M	T	W	T	F	S
			1	2	3	4
5	6	7	8	9	10	11
12	13	14	15	16	17	18
19	20	21	22	23	24	25
26	27	28	29	30	31	

MAY

S	M	T	W	T	F	S
	1	2	3	4	5	6
7	8	9	10	11	12	13
14	15	16	17	18	19	20
21	22	23	24	25	26	27
28	29	30	31			

CATCH YOUR BREATH

The word *stress* has an interesting etymology, coming in part from words meaning "narrowness," "oppression," and "drawn tight." So it makes sense that when you're under stress, you may feel as if the walls are closing in on you, as if your chest is drawn tight. It's almost hard to breathe.

On the one hand, there is stress, a sense of suffocation. On the other hand, there is God. The key is to remember God in the midst of your stress. To remember He is listening and ready to rescue you, to help you catch your breath. He'll do it every time. His job is to be there for you. Your job is to reach out for Him.

Help me catch my breath, Lord!

GOALS for this MONTH

- [ ] ....
- [ ] ....
- [ ] ....
- [ ] ....
- [ ] ....
- [ ] ....
- [ ] ....
- [ ] ....
- [ ] ....
- [ ] ....
- [ ] ....
- [ ] ....

Is anyone crying for help? GOD is listening, ready to rescue you. If your heart is broken, you'll find GOD right there; if you're kicked in the gut, he'll help you catch your breath. Disciples so often get into trouble; still, GOD is there every time.

PSALM 34:17–19 MSG

APRIL 2023

You amaze me, Lord, with how quickly
You respond to my cry. I thank You
for giving me strength!

SUNDAY, April 2   *Palm Sunday*

....

....

....

....

MONDAY, April 3

....

....

....

....

TUESDAY, April 4

....

....

....

....

WEDNESDAY, April 5   *Passover Begins at Sundown*

....

....

....

....

THURSDAY, April 6

....

....

....

....

FRIDAY, April 7   *Good Friday*

....

....

....

....

SATURDAY, April 8

....

....

....

....

> *I give you thanks, O LORD, with my whole*
> *heart.... On the day I called, you answered*
> *me; my strength of soul you increased.*
> PSALM 138:1, 3 ESV

Lord, one thing that keeps me going is
knowing I'm not alone. You are forever with
me, loving me, helping me, rescuing me.

SUNDAY, April 9 *Easter*

....
....
....
....

MONDAY, April 10

....
....
....
....

TUESDAY, April 11

....
....
....
....

WEDNESDAY, April 12

THURSDAY, April 13

FRIDAY, April 14

SATURDAY, April 15

No one stood by me. They all ran like scared rabbits. But it doesn't matter—the Master stood by me and helped me. . . . God's looking after me, keeping me safe in the kingdom of heaven.
2 TIMOTHY 4:16–18 MSG

APRIL 2023

As I begin each new day, Lord, I'll look for You
and Your power to do something amazing
in my life. My eyes are fixed on You!

SUNDAY, April 16

MONDAY, April 17

TUESDAY, April 18

WEDNESDAY, April 19

THURSDAY, April 20

FRIDAY, April 21

SATURDAY, April 22

Seeing Peter and John about to go into the temple, he asked to receive alms. And Peter directed his gaze at him, as did John, and said, "Look at us." And he fixed his attention on them, expecting to receive something from them.

ACTS 3:3–5 ESV

APRIL 2023

I praise You, Lord, for all You have
done and are doing in my life!

SUNDAY, April 23

MONDAY, April 24

TUESDAY, April 25

WEDNESDAY, April 26

THURSDAY, April 27

FRIDAY, April 28

SATURDAY, April 29

She said, "This time I'll praise GOD."
So she named him Judah (Praise-GOD).
GENESIS 29:35 MSG

MAY 2023

SUNDAY	MONDAY	TUESDAY	WEDNESDAY
30	1	2	3
7	8	9	10
14	15	16	17
Mother's Day			
21	22	23	24
28	29	30	31
	Memorial Day		

THURSDAY	FRIDAY	SATURDAY
4	5	6
National Day of Prayer		
11	12	13
18	19	20
25	26	27
1	2	3

APRIL

S	M	T	W	T	F	S
						1
2	3	4	5	6	7	8
9	10	11	12	13	14	15
16	17	18	19	20	21	22
23	24	25	26	27	28	29
30						

JUNE

S	M	T	W	T	F	S
				1	2	3
4	5	6	7	8	9	10
11	12	13	14	15	16	17
18	19	20	21	22	23	24
25	26	27	28	29	30	

FROM STRESS TO STRENGTH

Within you lies all the power required to turn your stress into strength and, in turn, your mourning into dancing (see Psalm 30:11). But first you have to believe that the same power that resurrected Jesus is alive and working in you! That it is unlimited, unassailable, unbelievable!

Thousands of years ago, the apostle Paul prayed that God would give you spiritual wisdom and insight to know Him better and realize the amazing power available to you.

Look for it. Express it. Move out of your stress and into God's strength—and dance!

With Your Spirit within me, Lord, I can do all You've called me to do. Keep this fact before me as I move from stress to strength.

GOALS for this MONTH

- [ ] ....
- [ ] ....
- [ ] ....
- [ ] ....
- [ ] ....
- [ ] ....
- [ ] ....
- [ ] ....
- [ ] ....
- [ ] ....
- [ ] ....
- [ ] ....

This is my prayer. That God. . .will give you spiritual wisdom and the insight to know more of him: that you may receive that inner illumination of the spirit which will make you realise how great is the hope to which he is calling you. . .and how tremendous is the power available to us who believe in God.

EPHESIANS 1:17–19 PHILLIPS

Lord, help me change my mindset
from my lack to Your plenty.

SUNDAY, April 30

MONDAY, May 1

TUESDAY, May 2

WEDNESDAY, May 3

THURSDAY, May 4   *National Day of Prayer*

FRIDAY, May 5

SATURDAY, May 6

Every beast of the forest is Mine, and the
cattle upon a thousand hills or upon the
mountains where thousands are.
PSALM 50:10 AMPC

MAY 2023

Thank You, Lord, for the spirit
of power and calm in You.

SUNDAY, May 7

MONDAY, May 8

TUESDAY, May 9

WEDNESDAY, May 10

THURSDAY, May 11

FRIDAY, May 12

SATURDAY, May 13

God did not give us a spirit of timidity (of cowardice, of craven and cringing and fawning fear), but [He has given us a spirit] of power and of love and of calm and well-balanced mind and discipline and self-control.

2 TIMOTHY 1:7 AMPC

MAY 2023

God of my heart and soul, hold my
hand. Lead me. I am Your child.

SUNDAY, May 14   *Mother's Day*

....

....

....

....

MONDAY, May 15

....

....

....

....

TUESDAY, May 16

....

....

....

....

WEDNESDAY, May 17

THURSDAY, May 18

FRIDAY, May 19

SATURDAY, May 20

Jesus called a little child to his side. . . .
"Believe me," he said, "unless you change your
whole outlook and become like little children
you will never enter the kingdom of Heaven."
MATTHEW 18:2–3 PHILLIPS

MAY 2023

Lord, I come to You, looking
to set my pace with Yours.

SUNDAY, May 21

MONDAY, May 22

TUESDAY, May 23

WEDNESDAY, May 24

....

....

....

....

THURSDAY, May 25

....

....

....

....

FRIDAY, May 26

....

....

....

....

SATURDAY, May 27

....

....

....

....

> *"May GOD, our very own God. . .keep us centered and devoted to him, following the life path he has cleared, watching the signposts, walking at the pace and rhythms he laid down for our ancestors."*
> 1 KINGS 8:57–58 MSG

At this point, Jesus, I'm not sure what—or who—people see when they look at me. So I'm coming to spend time with You, imbibing Your peace, strength, boldness, and so much more. May I grow each day to look more like You than anything or anyone else.

SUNDAY, May 28

MONDAY, May 29   *Memorial Day*

TUESDAY, May 30

WEDNESDAY, May 31

....
....
....
....

THURSDAY, June 1

....
....
....
....

FRIDAY, June 2

....
....
....
....

SATURDAY, June 3

....
....
....
....

Now when they saw the boldness of Peter and
John, and perceived that they were uneducated,
common men, they were astonished. And they
recognized that they had been with Jesus.
ACTS 4:13 ESV

JUNE 2023

SUNDAY	MONDAY	TUESDAY	WEDNESDAY
28	29	30	31
4	5	6	7
11	12	13	14 *Flag Day*
18 *Father's Day*	19	20	21 *First Day of Summer*
25	26	27	28

THURSDAY	FRIDAY	SATURDAY
1	2	3
8	9	10
15	16	17
22	23	24
29	30	1

MAY

S	M	T	W	T	F	S
	1	2	3	4	5	6
7	8	9	10	11	12	13
14	15	16	17	18	19	20
21	22	23	24	25	26	27
28	29	30	31			

JULY

S	M	T	W	T	F	S
						1
2	3	4	5	6	7	8
9	10	11	12	13	14	15
16	17	18	19	20	21	22
23	24	25	26	27	28	29
30	31					

HER PART, HIS PART

Feeling as if the whole world is on your shoulders? Thinking if you don't do it, it won't get done? Stop and consider that those feelings and thoughts are lies. For you have a God who is in it with you all the way. In fact, He wants you to know there are two parts to consider in your life—yours and His.

Your part is to immerse yourself in God's Word, pray, welcome His Spirit, expect the Lord is acting on your behalf, and leave the results to Him. His part is to work wonders.

Lord, help me to do what You would have me do and leave the rest to You.

GOALS for this MONTH

- ☐ ....
- ☐ ....
- ☐ ....
- ☐ ....
- ☐ ....
- ☐ ....
- ☐ ....
- ☐ ....
- ☐ ....
- ☐ ....
- ☐ ....

"Now, Lord. . .grant to your servants to continue to speak your word with all boldness, while you stretch out your hand to heal, and signs and wonders are performed through the name of your holy servant Jesus." And when they had prayed . . .they were all filled with the Holy Spirit and continued to speak the word of God with boldness.

ACTS 4:29–31 ESV

Help me steer clear of distractions, Lord,
and keep my feet firmly on Your path.

SUNDAY, June 4

MONDAY, June 5

TUESDAY, June 6

WEDNESDAY, June 7

THURSDAY, June 8

FRIDAY, June 9

SATURDAY, June 10

> *Josiah. . .began his thirty-one-year reign*
> *in Jerusalem. . . . He did right in the sight*
> *of the Lord. . .and turned not aside to*
> *the right hand or to the left.*
> 2 KINGS 22:1-2 AMPC

JUNE 2023

Control the tides of my mind, Lord,
so my joy will be in You alone.

SUNDAY, June 11

MONDAY, June 12

TUESDAY, June 13

WEDNESDAY, June 14   *Flag Day*

THURSDAY, June 15

FRIDAY, June 16

SATURDAY, June 17

*Now ask and keep on asking and you
will receive, so that your joy (gladness,
delight) may be full and complete.*
JOHN 16:24 AMPC

JUNE 2023

Lord, I'm here, seeking You above all else.
My new course is to set my heart on You.

SUNDAY, June 18   *Father's Day*

. . . .

MONDAY, June 19

. . . .

TUESDAY, June 20

. . . .

WEDNESDAY, June 21   *First Day of Summer*

THURSDAY, June 22

FRIDAY, June 23

SATURDAY, June 24

*"So don't worry and don't keep saying, 'What
shall we eat...drink or...wear?'... Set your heart
on the kingdom and his goodness, and all these
things will come to you as a matter of course."*
MATTHEW 6:31, 33 PHILLIPS

JUNE–JULY 2023

Thank You, God, for feeding me, healing
me with the power of Your Word.

SUNDAY, June 25

MONDAY, June 26

TUESDAY, June 27

WEDNESDAY, June 28

THURSDAY, June 29

FRIDAY, June 30

SATURDAY, July 1

My child, pay attention to what I say.
Listen carefully to my words. Don't lose sight
of them. Let them penetrate deep into your
heart, for they bring life to those who find
them, and healing to their whole body.
PROVERBS 4:20–22 NLT

JULY 2023

SUNDAY	MONDAY	TUESDAY	WEDNESDAY
25	26	27	28
2	3	4 *Independence Day*	5
9	10	11	12
16	17	18	19
23 / 30	24 / 31	25	26

THURSDAY	FRIDAY	SATURDAY
29	30	1
6	7	8
13	14	15
20	21	22
27	28	29

JUNE

S	M	T	W	T	F	S
				1	2	3
4	5	6	7	8	9	10
11	12	13	14	15	16	17
18	19	20	21	22	23	24
25	26	27	28	29	30	

AUGUST

S	M	T	W	T	F	S
		1	2	3	4	5
6	7	8	9	10	11	12
13	14	15	16	17	18	19
20	21	22	23	24	25	26
27	28	29	30	31		

CHANGE AGENT

Want to have some change in your life, live more in God's world than the one you've created for yourself? Tap into the power of the Holy Spirit. He's the change agent who will bring you around to where God desires you to be. He's as close as a breath, as near as a prayer. He's the gift of the One who loved you so much He died for you on the cross.

He's not only your Comforter, Counselor, Motivator, and Life Source. He's the One who'll change your attitude (see Romans 12:2) and your altitude, drawing you ever closer to the God of your heart, mind, body, and soul.

Lord, I'm ready for a change in my life. Help me to handle it, drawing ever closer to You in the process.

GOALS for this MONTH

- [ ] ....
- [ ] ....
- [ ] ....
- [ ] ....
- [ ] ....
- [ ] ....
- [ ] ....
- [ ] ....
- [ ] ....
- [ ] ....
- [ ] ....
- [ ] ....

*Be careful how you live. . . . Make the most of
every opportunity. . . . Don't act thoughtlessly,
but understand what the Lord wants you
to do. . . . Be filled with the Holy Spirit. . .
making music to the Lord in your hearts.*

EPHESIANS 5:15–19 NLT

Lord, show me how to invest the gifts You've given me then leave the results to You alone.

SUNDAY, July 2

MONDAY, July 3

TUESDAY, July 4   *Independence Day*

WEDNESDAY, July 5

THURSDAY, July 6

FRIDAY, July 7

SATURDAY, July 8

" 'Well done!' the king exclaimed. 'You are
a good servant. You have been faithful
with the little I entrusted to you.' "

LUKE 19:17 NLT

I'm tired of worrying about what other people think about who I am, what I do. I want You, Lord, to be my one and only influence. Stream Your guiding Spirit upon me.

SUNDAY, July 9

MONDAY, July 10

TUESDAY, July 11

WEDNESDAY, July 12

THURSDAY, July 13

FRIDAY, July 14

SATURDAY, July 15

"Teacher," they said, "we know that you speak and teach what is right and are not influenced by what others think. You teach the way of God truthfully."

LUKE 20:21 NLT

> Lord, may my confidence in You
> be my source of quiet power.

SUNDAY, July 16

MONDAY, July 17

TUESDAY, July 18

WEDNESDAY, July 19

THURSDAY, July 20

FRIDAY, July 21

SATURDAY, July 22

*In quietness and in [trusting]
confidence shall be your strength.*
ISAIAH 30:15 AMPC

JULY 2023

Lord, help me to slow down in
my thoughts and actions, knowing all
things will get done in Your time.

SUNDAY, July 23

....

....

....

....

MONDAY, July 24

....

....

....

....

TUESDAY, July 25

....

....

....

....

WEDNESDAY, July 26

THURSDAY, July 27

FRIDAY, July 28

SATURDAY, July 29

The thoughts of the [steadily] diligent tend only to plenteousness, but everyone who is impatient and hasty hastens only to want.
PROVERBS 21:5 AMPC

AUGUST 2023

SUNDAY	MONDAY	TUESDAY	WEDNESDAY
30	31	1	2
6	7	8	9
13	14	15	16
20	21	22	23
27	28	29	30

THURSDAY	FRIDAY	SATURDAY
3	4	5
10	11	12
17	18	19
24	25	26
31	1	2

"NEVERTHELESS. . ."

When you have God on your side, there is no need to stress and strain, even when people tell you your efforts will be useless. For God always has a "nevertheless" up His sleeve. His power can work through you when you stay in tune with His Spirit, allowing Him to rule your heart, mind, body, and soul. He will enable you to do above and beyond what you and others think you can do.

Let God's "nevertheless" ease your mind and strengthen your spirit. Know that God will build upon that which you accomplish in His power because, as He was with David, the God of hosts (see 2 Samuel 5:10) is with you.

Lord, help me see Your "nevertheless" in all the challenges I face and know that Your power is with me. In Jesus' name, amen.

GOALS for this MONTH

- [ ] ....
- [ ] ....
- [ ] ....
- [ ] ....
- [ ] ....
- [ ] ....
- [ ] ....
- [ ] ....
- [ ] ....
- [ ] ....
- [ ] ....
- [ ] ....

*The Jebusites, the inhabitants of the land. . .
said to David, "You will not come in here,
but the blind and the lame will ward you
off"—thinking, "David cannot come in here."
Nevertheless, David took the stronghold of Zion.*

2 Samuel 5:6–7 esv

Let's talk, Lord. Be my center!

SUNDAY, July 30

MONDAY, July 31

TUESDAY, August 1

WEDNESDAY, August 2

....

....

....

....

THURSDAY, August 3

....

....

....

....

FRIDAY, August 4

....

....

....

....

SATURDAY, August 5

....

....

....

....

Let petitions and praises shape your worries into prayers, letting God know your concerns. Before you know it, a sense of God's wholeness, everything coming together for good, will come and settle you down. It's wonderful what happens when Christ displaces worry at the center of your life.

PHILIPPIANS 4:6–7 MSG

AUGUST 2023

I place myself in Your loving care, Lord.
Watch me through the night.

SUNDAY, August 6

MONDAY, August 7

TUESDAY, August 8

WEDNESDAY, August 9

THURSDAY, August 10

FRIDAY, August 11

SATURDAY, August 12

In peace I will both lie down and sleep,
for You, Lord, alone make me dwell
in safety and confident trust.
PSALM 4:8 AMPC

Lord, help me become more aware
of my thoughts. Help me change them
to match Your way of thinking.

SUNDAY, August 13

MONDAY, August 14

TUESDAY, August 15

WEDNESDAY, August 16

THURSDAY, August 17

FRIDAY, August 18

SATURDAY, August 19

*"For my thoughts are not your thoughts,
neither are your ways my ways, declares the
LORD. For as the heavens are higher than the
earth, so are my ways higher than your ways
and my thoughts than your thoughts."*
ISAIAH 55:8–9 ESV

AUGUST 2023

I'm wholeheartedly embracing this God-life, Lord! I'm claiming Your promises and watching my stress sink into the sea.

SUNDAY, August 20

MONDAY, August 21

TUESDAY, August 22

WEDNESDAY, August 23

THURSDAY, August 24

FRIDAY, August 25

SATURDAY, August 26

"Embrace this God-life. . .and nothing will be too much for you. This mountain, for instance: Just say, 'Go jump in the lake'—no shuffling or hemming or hawing—and it's as good as done. That's why I urge you to pray for absolutely everything."

MARK 11:23–24 MSG

AUGUST-SEPTEMBER 2022

Help me, Lord, to see You standing
beside me in every challenge I face.

SUNDAY, August 27

MONDAY, August 28

TUESDAY, August 29

WEDNESDAY, August 30

THURSDAY, August 31

FRIDAY, September 1

SATURDAY, September 2

*They brought the Israelites an evil report of
the land which they had scouted out, saying,
The land through which we went to spy it
out is a land that devours its inhabitants.*

NUMBERS 13:32 AMPC

SEPTEMBER 2023

SUNDAY	MONDAY	TUESDAY	WEDNESDAY
27	28	29	30
3	4 *Labor Day*	5	6
10	11	12	13
17	18	19	20
24	25	26	27

THURSDAY	FRIDAY	SATURDAY
31	1	2
7	8	9
14	15	16
21	22	23 *First Day of Autumn*
28	29	30

AUGUST

S	M	T	W	T	F	S
		1	2	3	4	5
6	7	8	9	10	11	12
13	14	15	16	17	18	19
20	21	22	23	24	25	26
27	28	29	30	31		

OCTOBER

S	M	T	W	T	F	S
1	2	3	4	5	6	7
8	9	10	11	12	13	14
15	16	17	18	19	20	21
22	23	24	25	26	27	28
29	30	31				

ZEROING IN

Stress can come upon us when we find ourselves running after a million different things, unable (or unwilling) to zero in on exactly what we want. When Jesus encountered a blind beggar calling out His name, He stopped and asked him, "What do you want Me to do for you?" Although Jesus knew the man wanted sight not alms, He made no move until the beggar said to Him: "Master, let me receive my sight" (Mark 10:51 AMPC). "And Jesus said to him, Go your way; your faith has healed you. And at once he received his sight and accompanied Jesus on the road" (Mark 10:52 AMPC).

Take some time now to stop and consider: What do you really want Jesus to do for you? Then pray and go your way, and your faith will heal you as you follow Jesus down the road.

Lord, help me to zero in on what I really want, then trust in You as I follow Your pathway.

GOALS for this MONTH

- [ ] ....
- [ ] ....
- [ ] ....
- [ ] ....
- [ ] ....
- [ ] ....
- [ ] ....
- [ ] ....
- [ ] ....
- [ ] ....
- [ ] ....
- [ ] ....
- [ ] ....

*And Jesus said to him, What do
you want Me to do for you?*
MARK 10:51 AMPC

SEPTEMBER 2023

I know I am nothing without You, Lord.
So I come to You now for the strength
to do what You have called me to do.

SUNDAY, September 3

MONDAY, September 4   *Labor Day*

TUESDAY, September 5

WEDNESDAY, September 6

THURSDAY, September 7

FRIDAY, September 8

SATURDAY, September 9

*I have strength for all things in Christ
Who empowers me [I am ready for anything
and equal to anything through Him Who
infuses inner strength into me; I am self-
sufficient in Christ's sufficiency].*

PHILIPPIANS 4:13 AMPC

SEPTEMBER 2023

Lord, bring to my mind those I need to forgive,
and help me to do so in this moment.

SUNDAY, September 10

MONDAY, September 11

TUESDAY, September 12

WEDNESDAY, September 13

THURSDAY, September 14

FRIDAY, September 15

SATURDAY, September 16

Clothe yourselves with tenderhearted mercy,
kindness, humility, gentleness, and patience.
Make allowance for each other's faults, and
forgive anyone who offends you. Remember, the
Lord forgave you, so you must forgive others.
COLOSSIANS 3:12–13 NLT

SEPTEMBER 2023

I know I'll see Your goodness in
this world and in my life, Lord!

SUNDAY, September 17

MONDAY, September 18

TUESDAY, September 19

WEDNESDAY, September 20

THURSDAY, September 21

FRIDAY, September 22

SATURDAY, September 23 *First Day of Autumn*

[What, what would have become of me] had I not believed that I would see the Lord's goodness in the land of the living! Wait and hope for and expect the Lord; be brave and of good courage and let your heart be stout and enduring.

PSALM 27:13–14 AMPC

SEPTEMBER 2023

Lord, I am counting on You, trusting
You are holding me in Your hand. Help
me to rest secure in that knowledge.

SUNDAY, September 24

MONDAY, September 25

TUESDAY, September 26

WEDNESDAY, September 27

....

....

....

....

THURSDAY, September 28

....

....

....

....

FRIDAY, September 29

....

....

....

....

SATURDAY, September 30

....

....

....

....

Trust (lean on, rely on, and be confident)
in the Lord and do good; so shall you
dwell in the land and feed surely on His
faithfulness, and truly you shall be fed.
PSALM 37:3 AMPC

OCTOBER 2023

SUNDAY	MONDAY	TUESDAY	WEDNESDAY
1	2	3	4
8	9 *Columbus Day*	10	11
15	16	17	18
22	23	24	25
29	30	31 *Halloween*	1

THURSDAY	FRIDAY	SATURDAY
5	6	7
12	13	14
19	20	21
26	27	28
2	3	4

SEPTEMBER

S	M	T	W	T	F	S
					1	2
3	4	5	6	7	8	9
10	11	12	13	14	15	16
17	18	19	20	21	22	23
24	25	26	27	28	29	30

NOVEMBER

S	M	T	W	T	F	S
			1	2	3	4
5	6	7	8	9	10	11
12	13	14	15	16	17	18
19	20	21	22	23	24	25
26	27	28	29	30		

TRUE DELIGHT

It's easy to get stressed out, pulled in a thousand different ways as we try to fulfill our own desires or those of other people. In the quest to "satisfy" ourselves or others, our true path is obscured. Then when we actually obtain what we (or others) desire, we find that either it doesn't satisfy or another desire is just around the corner, and we begin the chase all over again.

God wants you to realize the only desire that can give you true rest and peace in this life is delighting yourself in Him, making closeness and fellowship with Him your only goal. Doing so not only will put all your other desires in their rightful place as your wants begin to line up with His, but it will give you rest from chasing the seemingly never-ending wants.

Lord, I'm setting myself down, giving myself time to just rest and take pleasure in You—my true delight and desire.

GOALS for this MONTH

- [ ] ....
- [ ] ....
- [ ] ....
- [ ] ....
- [ ] ....
- [ ] ....
- [ ] ....
- [ ] ....
- [ ] ....
- [ ] ....
- [ ] ....
- [ ] ....
- [ ] ....

*Delight yourself also in the Lord, and He will give
you the desires and secret petitions of your heart.*

PSALM 37:4 AMPC

OCTOBER 2023

Lord, I'm committing my way to You,
knowing You will bring out the best in me.

SUNDAY, October 1

MONDAY, October 2

TUESDAY, October 3

WEDNESDAY, October 4

THURSDAY, October 5

FRIDAY, October 6

SATURDAY, October 7

Commit your way to the Lord [roll and repose each care of your load on Him]; trust (lean on, rely on, and be confident) also in Him and He will bring it to pass.

PSALM 37:5 AMPC

OCTOBER 2023

Lord, here I am, leaning back upon You,
listening to Your breath as it aligns with mine.
Fill me with peace beyond understanding as I
commit my path and desires to You, trusting
and delighting in You and Your love.

SUNDAY, October 8

....
....
....
....

MONDAY, October 9   *Columbus Day*

....
....
....
....

TUESDAY, October 10

....
....
....
....

WEDNESDAY, October 11

THURSDAY, October 12

FRIDAY, October 13

SATURDAY, October 14

Be still and rest in the Lord; wait for Him and patiently lean yourself upon Him; fret not yourself because of him who prospers in his way.

PSALM 37:7 AMPC

OCTOBER 2023

Lord, help me to do what I can and then leave
the rest in Your amazingly capable hands.

SUNDAY, October 15

MONDAY, October 16

TUESDAY, October 17

WEDNESDAY, October 18

....

....

....

....

THURSDAY, October 19

....

....

....

....

FRIDAY, October 20

....

....

....

....

SATURDAY, October 21

....

....

....

....

"She did what she could when she could."
MARK 14:8 MSG

OCTOBER 2023

*I need not fear because I know
You are for me, God. I praise You
and the power of Your Word!*

SUNDAY, October 22

MONDAY, October 23

TUESDAY, October 24

WEDNESDAY, October 25

THURSDAY, October 26

FRIDAY, October 27

SATURDAY, October 28

When I am afraid, I put my trust in you. In God, whose word I praise, in God I trust; I shall not be afraid. . . . This I know, that God is for me. In God, whose word I praise, in the LORD, whose word I praise, in God I trust; I shall not be afraid.

PSALM 56:3-4, 9-11 ESV

NOVEMBER 2023

SUNDAY	MONDAY	TUESDAY	WEDNESDAY
29	30	31	1
5 *Daylight Saving Time Ends*	6	7 *Election Day*	8
12	13	14	15
19	20	21	22
26	27	28	29

THURSDAY	FRIDAY	SATURDAY
2	3	4
9	10	11 *Veterans Day*
16	17	18
23	24 *Thanksgiving Day*	25
30	1	2

OCTOBER

S	M	T	W	T	F	S
1	2	3	4	5	6	7
8	9	10	11	12	13	14
15	16	17	18	19	20	21
22	23	24	25	26	27	28
29	30	31				

DECEMBER

S	M	T	W	T	F	S
					1	2
3	4	5	6	7	8	9
10	11	12	13	14	15	16
17	18	19	20	21	22	23
24	25	26	27	28	29	30
31						

WEIGHED DOWN

Proverbs 12:25 (AMPC) says, "Anxiety in a man's heart weighs it down." So what are we to do with our worries and stresses that have become so burdensome we are stooped low and feel we can no longer breathe? God wants us to come to Him every day—or every moment of every day, if needed—and leave all that weight on our hearts in His hands. When we do, He may not remove us from whatever situation we find ourselves in, but He'll keep us strong and give us peace in the midst of it. And once our hearts, minds, and souls are no longer burdened, God will make sure no one and nothing will push us off the course He's set for our lives.

What anxiety is weighing you down? Give it to God then stand tall.

Lord, show me what burdens
I need to give to You.

GOALS for this MONTH

- [ ] ....
- [ ] ....
- [ ] ....
- [ ] ....
- [ ] ....
- [ ] ....
- [ ] ....
- [ ] ....
- [ ] ....
- [ ] ....
- [ ] ....
- [ ] ....
- [ ] ....

*Cast your burden on the Lord [releasing
the weight of it] and He will sustain you; He
will never allow the [consistently] righteous
to be moved (made to slip, fall, or fail).*

PSALM 55:22 AMPC

OCTOBER–NOVEMBER 2023

I'm rejoicing in the precious moments
You have given me today, Lord, and
keeping my eyes open for You!

SUNDAY, October 29

MONDAY, October 30

TUESDAY, October 31   *Halloween*

WEDNESDAY, November 1

....

....

....

....

THURSDAY, November 2

....

....

....

....

FRIDAY, November 3

....

....

....

....

SATURDAY, November 4

....

....

....

....

This is the day that the LORD has made;
let us rejoice and be glad in it.
PSALM 118:24 ESV

NOVEMBER 2023

I'm running to You, Lord, my Tower
of Power. For in You, I know I'm safe.

SUNDAY, November 5   *Daylight Saving Time Ends*

....

....

....

....

MONDAY, November 6

....

....

....

....

TUESDAY, November 7   *Election Day*

....

....

....

....

WEDNESDAY, November 8

THURSDAY, November 9

FRIDAY, November 10

SATURDAY, November 11   *Veterans Day*

The name of the Lord is a strong tower;
the [consistently] righteous man [upright
and in right standing with God] runs into it
and is safe, high [above evil] and strong.
PROVERBS 18:10 AMPC

NOVEMBER 2023

God, speak out of Your depths
and into mine. Reveal in Your Word
what You would have me know.

SUNDAY, November 12

MONDAY, November 13

TUESDAY, November 14

WEDNESDAY, November 15

THURSDAY, November 16

FRIDAY, November 17

SATURDAY, November 18

The God of heaven. . .gives wisdom to the wise and knowledge to those who have understanding! He reveals the deep and secret things; He knows what is in the darkness, and the light dwells with Him!

DANIEL 2:19, 21–22 AMPC

NOVEMBER 2023

Lord, I rest in the knowledge that
You will see me through all things, that
You will give me the strength I need to
live the life You've planned for me.

SUNDAY, November 19

....
....
....
....

MONDAY, November 20

....
....
....
....

TUESDAY, November 21

....
....
....
....

WEDNESDAY, November 22

THURSDAY, November 23   *Thanksgiving Day*

FRIDAY, November 24

SATURDAY, November 25

In my distress I cried out to the LORD; yes,
I prayed to my God for help. He heard me
from his sanctuary; my cry to him reached his
ears. . . . He reached down from heaven and
rescued me; he drew me out of deep waters.
PSALM 18:6, 16 NLT

Help me, Holy Spirit, to be in harmony with
Your will, Your agenda—Your plans, not mine.
Keep me at the center of God's love.

SUNDAY, November 26

....
....
....
....

MONDAY, November 27

....
....
....
....

TUESDAY, November 28

....
....
....
....

WEDNESDAY, November 29

THURSDAY, November 30

FRIDAY, December 1

SATURDAY, December 2

Carefully build yourselves up in this most holy faith by praying in the Holy Spirit, staying right at the center of God's love, keeping your arms open and outstretched, ready for the mercy of our Master, Jesus Christ. This is the unending life, the real life!

JUDE 1:20–21 MSG

DECEMBER 2023

SUNDAY	MONDAY	TUESDAY	WEDNESDAY
26	27	28	29
3	4	5	6
10	11	12	13
17	18	19	20
24 *Christmas Eve*	25	26	27
New Year's Eve 31	*Christmas Day*		

THURSDAY	FRIDAY	SATURDAY
30	1	2
7 *Hanukkah Begins at Sundown*	8	9
14	15	16
21 *First Day of Winter*	22	23
28	29	30

CALLING GOD

You never know when God is going to reveal something to you, some truth you need to know, some secret to help you connect the dots, see His hand, discover the solution, find some hope. And God can deliver that message no matter where you are! (Jeremiah received the words of 33:3 while he was locked up in jail!) But you have to call on God. You have to pray to Him. When you do, He'll answer you, telling you things you otherwise would never know! He—the Creator of the universe, the One who knows how everything works—will help you figure things out.

The formula is simple: Call. Pray. Listen. Then marvel at the wonder of the knowledge of God.

Dear Lord, here I am! Speak! Tell me what You'd have me know.

GOALS for this MONTH

- [ ] ....
- [ ] ....
- [ ] ....
- [ ] ....
- [ ] ....
- [ ] ....
- [ ] ....
- [ ] ....
- [ ] ....
- [ ] ....
- [ ] ....
- [ ] ....

"This is GOD's Message, the God who made earth, made it livable and lasting, known everywhere as GOD: 'Call to me and I will answer you. I'll tell you marvelous and wondrous things that you could never figure out on your own.' "

JEREMIAH 33:3 MSG

DECEMBER 2023

I'm not sure, Lord, why things don't always
work out, but I know You have a plan.
So I'm ready, Lord. Where to next?

SUNDAY, December 3

MONDAY, December 4

TUESDAY, December 5

WEDNESDAY, December 6

THURSDAY, December 7 *Hanukkah Begins at Sundown*

FRIDAY, December 8

SATURDAY, December 9

GOD addressed Samuel: "So, how long are you going to mope over Saul? You know I've rejected him as king over Israel. Fill your flask with anointing oil and get going. I'm sending you to Jesse of Bethlehem. I've spotted the very king I want among his sons."

1 SAMUEL 16:1 MSG

DECEMBER 2023

I'm trusting in Your timing,
Lord. Bless my faith.

SUNDAY, December 10

....

....

....

MONDAY, December 11

....

....

....

TUESDAY, December 12

....

....

....

....

WEDNESDAY, December 13

THURSDAY, December 14

FRIDAY, December 15

SATURDAY, December 16

*But God remembered Noah and all the
beasts and all the livestock that were with
him in the ark. And God made a wind blow
over the earth, and the waters subsided.*

GENESIS 8:1 ESV

DECEMBER 2023

I'm depending on You, Lord, for all I need. You've brought me out of the depths of despair so many times before. Do so again as I lean back on You.

SUNDAY, December 17

MONDAY, December 18

TUESDAY, December 19

WEDNESDAY, December 20

THURSDAY, December 21   *First Day of Winter*

FRIDAY, December 22

SATURDAY, December 23

We're depending on GOD; he's everything we need.
What's more, our hearts brim with joy since we've
taken for our own his holy name. Love us, GOD, with
all you've got—that's what we're depending on.
PSALM 33:20–21 MSG

DECEMBER 2023

Lord, I come seeking Your face,
craving Your presence above all else.
Give me the peace only You can give.
Then strengthen my hands to do Your will.

SUNDAY, December 24 *Christmas Eve*

MONDAY, December 25 *Christmas Day*

TUESDAY, December 26

WEDNESDAY, December 27

....
....
....
....

THURSDAY, December 28

....
....
....
....

FRIDAY, December 29

....
....
....
....

SATURDAY, December 30

....
....
....
....

If you seek Him [inquiring for and of Him, craving Him as your soul's first necessity], He will be found by you.

2 CHRONICLES 15:2 AMPC

Lord, You're my Keeper, constantly tending
to me, protecting me. Help me to bloom
where You've planted me—for Your glory!

SUNDAY, December 31 *New Year's Eve*

MONDAY, January 1 *New Year's Day*

TUESDAY, January 2

WEDNESDAY, January 3

THURSDAY, January 4

FRIDAY, January 5

SATURDAY, January 6

I, the Lord, am its Keeper; I water it
every moment; lest anyone harm it,
I guard and keep it night and day.
ISAIAH 27:3 AMPC

CONTACTS

Name:

Address:

Phone:

Email:

Name:

Address:

Phone:

Email:

Name:

Address:

Phone:

Email:

Name:

Address:

Phone:

Email:

Name:

Address:

Phone:

Email:

CONTACTS

Name:

Address:

Phone:

Email:

Name:

Address:

Phone:

Email:

Name:

Address:

Phone:

Email:

Name:

Address:

Phone:

Email:

Name:

Address:

Phone:

Email:

CONTACTS

Name:

Address:

Phone:

Email:

Name:

Address:

Phone:

Email:

Name:

Address:

Phone:

Email:

Name:

Address:

Phone:

Email:

Name:

Address:

Phone:

Email:

CONTACTS

Name:

Address:

Phone:

Email:

Name:

Address:

Phone:

Email:

Name:

Address:

Phone:

Email:

Name:

Address:

Phone:

Email:

Name:

Address:

Phone:

Email:

CONTACTS

Name:

Address:

Phone:

Email:

Name:

Address:

Phone:

Email:

Name:

Address:

Phone:

Email:

Name:

Address:

Phone:

Email:

Name:

Address:

Phone:

Email:

CONTACTS

Name:

Address:

Phone:

Email:

Name:

Address:

Phone:

Email:

Name:

Address:

Phone:

Email:

Name:

Address:

Phone:

Email:

Name:

Address:

Phone:

Email:

CONTACTS

Name:

Address:

Phone:

Email:

Name:

Address:

Phone:

Email:

Name:

Address:

Phone:

Email:

Name:

Address:

Phone:

Email:

Name:

Address:

Phone:

Email:

CONTACTS

Name:
....
Address:
....
Phone:
....
Email:

Name:
....
Address:
....
Phone:
....
Email:

Name:
....
Address:
....
Phone:
....
Email:

Name:
....
Address:
....
Phone:
....
Email:

Name:
....
Address:
....
Phone:
....
Email:

CONTACTS

Name:

Address:

Phone:

Email:

Name:

Address:

Phone:

Email:

Name:

Address:

Phone:

Email:

Name:

Address:

Phone:

Email:

Name:

Address:

Phone:

Email:

CONTACTS

Name:

Address:

Phone:

Email:

Name:

Address:

Phone:

Email:

Name:

Address:

Phone:

Email:

Name:

Address:

Phone:

Email:

Name:

Address:

Phone:

Email:

CONTACTS

Name:

Address:

Phone:

Email:

Name:

Address:

Phone:

Email:

Name:

Address:

Phone:

Email:

Name:

Address:

Phone:

Email:

Name:

Address:

Phone:

Email:

CONTACTS

Name:

Address:

Phone:

Email:

Name:

Address:

Phone:

Email:

Name:

Address:

Phone:

Email:

Name:

Address:

Phone:

Email:

Name:

Address:

Phone:

Email:

CONTACTS

Name:

Address:

Phone:

Email:

Name:

Address:

Phone:

Email:

Name:

Address:

Phone:

Email:

Name:

Address:

Phone:

Email:

Name:

Address:

Phone:

Email:

CONTACTS

Name:

Address:

Phone:

Email:

Name:

Address:

Phone:

Email:

Name:

Address:

Phone:

Email:

Name:

Address:

Phone:

Email:

Name:

Address:

Phone:

Email:

YEAR-AT-A-GLANCE CALENDARS

2024

JANUARY
S	M	T	W	T	F	S
	1	2	3	4	5	6
7	8	9	10	11	12	13
14	15	16	17	18	19	20
21	22	23	24	25	26	27
28	29	30	31			

FEBRUARY
S	M	T	W	T	F	S
				1	2	3
4	5	6	7	8	9	10
11	12	13	14	15	16	17
18	19	20	21	22	23	24
25	26	27	28	29		

MARCH
S	M	T	W	T	F	S
					1	2
3	4	5	6	7	8	9
10	11	12	13	14	15	16
17	18	19	20	21	22	23
24	25	26	27	28	29	30
31						

APRIL
S	M	T	W	T	F	S
	1	2	3	4	5	6
7	8	9	10	11	12	13
14	15	16	17	18	19	20
21	22	23	24	25	26	27
28	29	30				

MAY
S	M	T	W	T	F	S
			1	2	3	4
5	6	7	8	9	10	11
12	13	14	15	16	17	18
19	20	21	22	23	24	25
26	27	28	29	30	31	

JUNE
S	M	T	W	T	F	S
						1
2	3	4	5	6	7	8
9	10	11	12	13	14	15
16	17	18	19	20	21	22
23	24	25	26	27	28	29
30						

JULY
S	M	T	W	T	F	S
	1	2	3	4	5	6
7	8	9	10	11	12	13
14	15	16	17	18	19	20
21	22	23	24	25	26	27
28	29	30	31			

AUGUST
S	M	T	W	T	F	S
				1	2	3
4	5	6	7	8	9	10
11	12	13	14	15	16	17
18	19	20	21	22	23	24
25	26	27	28	29	30	31

SEPTEMBER
S	M	T	W	T	F	S
1	2	3	4	5	6	7
8	9	10	11	12	13	14
15	16	17	18	19	20	21
22	23	24	25	26	27	28
29	30					

OCTOBER
S	M	T	W	T	F	S
		1	2	3	4	5
6	7	8	9	10	11	12
13	14	15	16	17	18	19
20	21	22	23	24	25	26
27	28	29	30	31		

NOVEMBER
S	M	T	W	T	F	S
					1	2
3	4	5	6	7	8	9
10	11	12	13	14	15	16
17	18	19	20	21	22	23
24	25	26	27	28	29	30

DECEMBER
S	M	T	W	T	F	S
1	2	3	4	5	6	7
8	9	10	11	12	13	14
15	16	17	18	19	20	21
22	23	24	25	26	27	28
29	30	31				

2025

JANUARY
S	M	T	W	T	F	S
			1	2	3	4
5	6	7	8	9	10	11
12	13	14	15	16	17	18
19	20	21	22	23	24	25
26	27	28	29	30	31	

FEBRUARY
S	M	T	W	T	F	S
						1
2	3	4	5	6	7	8
9	10	11	12	13	14	15
16	17	18	19	20	21	22
23	24	25	26	27	28	

MARCH
S	M	T	W	T	F	S
						1
2	3	4	5	6	7	8
9	10	11	12	13	14	15
16	17	18	19	20	21	22
23	24	25	26	27	28	29
30	31					

APRIL
S	M	T	W	T	F	S
		1	2	3	4	5
6	7	8	9	10	11	12
13	14	15	16	17	18	19
20	21	22	23	24	25	26
27	28	29	30			

MAY
S	M	T	W	T	F	S
				1	2	3
4	5	6	7	8	9	10
11	12	13	14	15	16	17
18	19	20	21	22	23	24
25	26	27	28	29	30	31

JUNE
S	M	T	W	T	F	S
1	2	3	4	5	6	7
8	9	10	11	12	13	14
15	16	17	18	19	20	21
22	23	24	25	26	27	28
29	30					

JULY
S	M	T	W	T	F	S
		1	2	3	4	5
6	7	8	9	10	11	12
13	14	15	16	17	18	19
20	21	22	23	24	25	26
27	28	29	30	31		

AUGUST
S	M	T	W	T	F	S
					1	2
3	4	5	6	7	8	9
10	11	12	13	14	15	16
17	18	19	20	21	22	23
24	25	26	27	28	29	30
31						

SEPTEMBER
S	M	T	W	T	F	S
	1	2	3	4	5	6
7	8	9	10	11	12	13
14	15	16	17	18	19	20
21	22	23	24	25	26	27
28	29	30				

OCTOBER
S	M	T	W	T	F	S
			1	2	3	4
5	6	7	8	9	10	11
12	13	14	15	16	17	18
19	20	21	22	23	24	25
26	27	28	29	30	31	

NOVEMBER
S	M	T	W	T	F	S
						1
2	3	4	5	6	7	8
9	10	11	12	13	14	15
16	17	18	19	20	21	22
23	24	25	26	27	28	29
30						

DECEMBER
S	M	T	W	T	F	S
	1	2	3	4	5	6
7	8	9	10	11	12	13
14	15	16	17	18	19	20
21	22	23	24	25	26	27
28	29	30	31